920 BELL

what would you ask?

ALEXANDER GRAHAM BELL

Anita Ganeri
Illustrated by Rachael Phillips

Belitha Press

First published in the UK in 2000 by
Belitha Press Limited, London House,
Great Eastern Wharf, Parkgate Road,
London SW11 4NQ

ISBN 1 84138 134 9

British Library Cataloguing in Publication Data
for this book is available from the British Library.

Printed in Singapore

10 9 8 7 6 5 4 3 2 1

355279

Editor: Veronica Ross
Designer: Caroline Grimshaw
Illustrator: Rachael Phillips
Consultants: Hester Collicutt and Alison Porter

Contents

What do you do?

'I am a teacher and inventor. My most famous invention was the telephone.'

Today, the telephone is part of everyday life. Pick up a telephone, and press or dial a number and you can talk to a friend in the house next door or halfway around the world. We use the telephone so much that it is hard to imagine life without it.

Many people helped to invent the telephone, but the most important was Scottish-born teacher, Alexander Graham Bell. In 1876, Bell made the first telephone call from his workshop in Boston, USA. For years, he had dreamed of making a machine that could send the sound of a voice using electricity. Many people thought he was mad. But on 10 March 1876, Bell made his dream come true.

The telephone quickly caught on. Before long, people were talking by telephone across the USA and in many European countries. Today, millions of telephones link callers all over the world. The telephone brought Bell fame and fortune. It also changed the world.

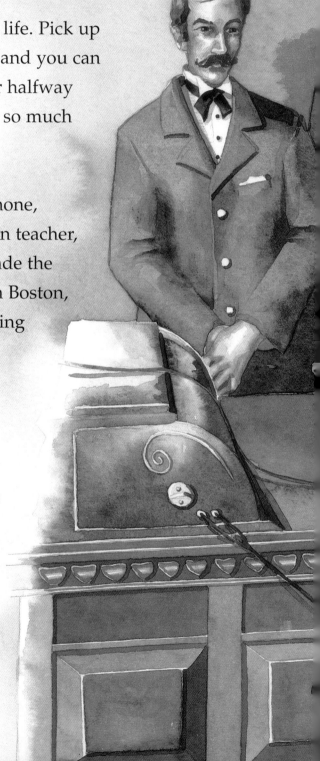

Where were you born?

'I was born in Edinburgh, Scotland.'

Alexander Bell was born on 3 March 1847 in South Charlotte Street, Edinburgh, Scotland. His father, Alexander Melville Bell, was a professor at Edinburgh University. Alexander and his two brothers, Melville and Edward, were looked after by their mother, Eliza.

Alexander's father was an expert in speech and elocution. He was also interested in helping people with hearing difficulties. It was often difficult for deaf people to speak clearly because they could not hear the sounds they were making.

When Alexander was 11 years old, a family friend called Alexander Graham came to visit. Young Alexander decided to adopt the middle name Graham and call himself Alexander Graham Bell, although his family always called him Aleck.

Did you like going to school?

'No, I did not! And I didn't stay for very long.'

Aleck and his brothers did not go to school. Instead, their mother taught them at home. Aleck was curious and interested in everything. He was especially keen on music and learned to play the piano when he was very young. He told his family that when he grew up he wanted to be a concert pianist.

When he was 11, Aleck was sent to the
Royal Edinburgh High School. It was
a very strict school. Aleck hated his
time there, and left after only two years
with no qualifications.

Aleck's father was not very pleased.
He sent Aleck to London to stay
with his grandfather who was
also a speech expert. Aleck loved
his grandfather and soon his
studies began to improve.
He also began to learn
how the human
voice worked.

Why did you become a teacher?

'I wanted to help people who could not hear properly to speak.'

Back in Edinburgh, Aleck decided to become a teacher. He applied for a job at Weston House Academy in Elgin, Scotland, where he taught music and elocution. It was lucky that Aleck looked older than he was. At 15 years old, he was younger than some of his pupils!

In 1865, the Bell family moved to London. For many years, Aleck's father had been working on a special type of alphabet called Visible Speech. It used symbols that stood for sounds. The symbols showed the positions that the tongue, mouth, lips and throat needed to be in to make a particular sound. Aleck became his father's assistant, helping him to teach Visible Speech to children with hearing and speech difficulties. It was a great success.

In 1867, Aleck's younger brother, Edward, fell ill with tuberculosis and died. He was only 17 years old. Three years later Aleck's older brother, Melville, also died from tuberculosis. Aleck's father decided to move to Canada where the climate was healthier. So on 21 July 1870 Aleck and his parents set sail to start their new life.

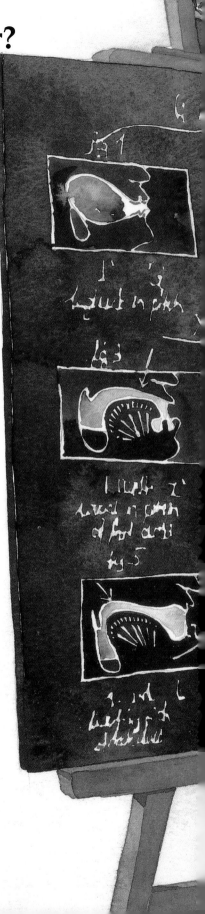

When did you work on your inventions?

'I taught during the day and worked
on my inventions at night.'

While his parents settled in Canada, Aleck
went to the United States. He worked in
Boston teaching at a new school for the deaf.
Aleck was a patient and dedicated teacher.
He was able to help many pupils
to speak using Visible Speech.

At night, Aleck carried on with his experiments. He had an idea for improving the design of the telegraph. At that time, the telegraph was the only way of sending a message over a long distance. The telegraph worked by turning letters into code. The code was then sent as bursts of electricity along wires. The problem was that only one message could be sent at a time and lines were always busy. Aleck was sure that there must be a way of sending several messages at once.

After a year of working day and night, Aleck was exhausted. He went to his parents' house in Canada for a well-earned rest.

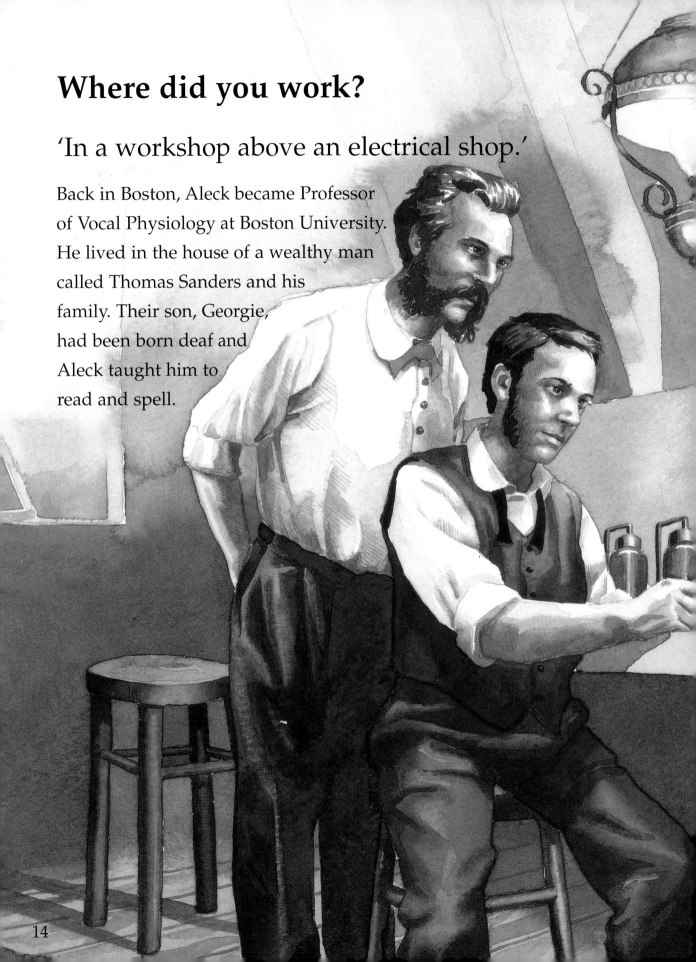

Where did you work?

'In a workshop above an electrical shop.'

Back in Boston, Aleck became Professor
of Vocal Physiology at Boston University.
He lived in the house of a wealthy man
called Thomas Sanders and his
family. Their son, Georgie,
had been born deaf and
Aleck taught him to
read and spell.

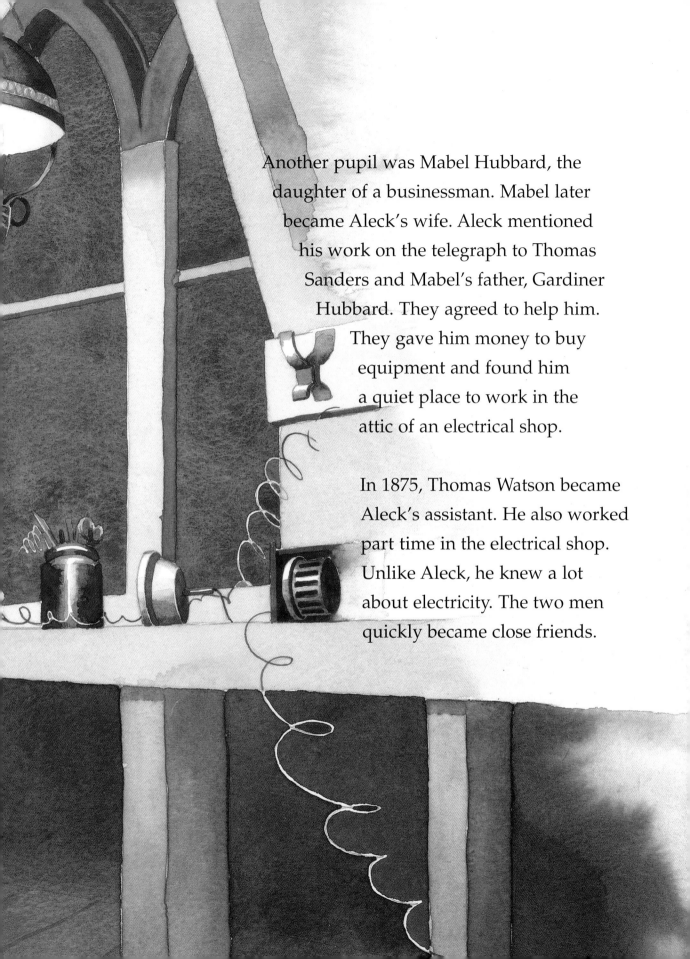

Another pupil was Mabel Hubbard, the daughter of a businessman. Mabel later became Aleck's wife. Aleck mentioned his work on the telegraph to Thomas Sanders and Mabel's father, Gardiner Hubbard. They agreed to help him. They gave him money to buy equipment and found him a quiet place to work in the attic of an electrical shop.

In 1875, Thomas Watson became Aleck's assistant. He also worked part time in the electrical shop. Unlike Aleck, he knew a lot about electricity. The two men quickly became close friends.

What was your greatest invention?

'A machine for sending electrical signals through wires. In other words, the telephone!'

For months, Aleck and Thomas Watson worked hard to improve the telegraph. But Aleck had another idea. He wanted to make a 'speaking telegraph', in other words, a telephone!

A telephone uses electricity flowing along wires, like a telegraph. But, instead of codes, it sends actual sounds. A telephone converts the sound of your voice into an electric current (in the mouthpiece), which is sent along the wire. At the other end, the telephone receiving the call will change the electric current back into sound.

Aleck knew that speaking makes the air vibrate in waves. But how could he turn sound waves into electricity? Then he had a brainwave. In the mouthpiece, he put a thin sheet of parchment, called a diaphragm, and an electromagnet. When you spoke into the mouthpiece, the sound waves hit the diaphragm and made it vibrate. Then the electromagnet turned the vibrations into electricity. At the other end, a similar device turned the electricity back into sound.

On 7 March 1876, Aleck was awarded US patent number 174, 465 one of the most famous patents in history. He was the official inventor of the telephone.

Who made the first telephone call?

'I did. But it happened by accident.'

Aleck had still not been able to send the sound of a voice clearly along his telephone. But that was about to change. Three days after he received his patent, the first telephone call was made.

It was Friday afternoon on 10 March 1876. Aleck was sitting in one room testing a transmitter. Wires connected it to a receiver in the next room where Thomas Watson was working. Just then, Aleck knocked over a bottle and spilt acid over his trousers. Without thinking, he shouted into his mouthpiece, 'Mr Watson, come here, I want to see you.' To his astonishment, Watson came into the room. He had heard Aleck's call for help over the telephone.

In great excitement, the two men took turns to speak into the telephone. At first, the sound was fuzzy and muffled. Then Aleck heard Watson ask, 'Mr Bell, do you understand what I say?' The words were loud and clear.

How did the telephone change your life?

'It made me famous all over the world. It also made my fortune.'

The telephone brought Aleck fame and fortune. But first he had to show it off. To begin with people were suspicious of the telephone. Some even thought it was a hoax. Aleck had to convince them that his invention could really change their lives.

In June 1876, Aleck showed his telephone at the great Centenary Exhibition in Philadelphia. It was the star of the show and won a medal. In July 1877, Aleck, Watson, Hubbard and Sanders set up the Bell Telephone Company to hire out telephones to the public.

July 1877 was a busy time for Aleck. He and Mabel Hubbard were married and travelled to Britain for their honeymoon. But there wasn't much time for rest. Everyone wanted to know about the telephone. Aleck was asked to give many demonstrations, including one to Queen Victoria.

Back in the USA, Aleck made a decision. The telephone had made him very wealthy, but it also took up a lot of his time. So, in 1880, Aleck left the Bell Telephone Company.

Did you invent anything else?

'Oh yes, I invented lots of other things.'

Aleck was only 32 years old. Now he had to decide what to do with his life. He knew that he wanted to carry on inventing. In 1880, he was awarded the Volta Prize by the French government. The prize was named after Alessandro Volta, the inventor of the battery. Aleck used the prize money to set up the Volta Laboratory in Washington DC. He wanted it to be an inventions factory where inventors could work on their ideas.

One of Aleck's favourite inventions was a machine called a photophone. It used light instead of electricity to send sounds. Aleck was so excited by it that he wanted to call his second daughter, Photophone, instead of Daisy!

Aleck's other inventions included a graphophone for recording and playing sounds, and a metal detector for finding bullets in people who had been shot. He also invented a respirator. This was a machine that helped people with breathing problems to breathe artificially.

Did you have any other hobbies?

'I was always busy doing something.'

In 1885, Aleck bought a summer home at Baddeck Bay on the island of Cape Breton, off Nova Scotia, Canada. Aleck loved the countryside. It reminded him of his childhood in Scotland. His family spent every summer at Cape Breton for almost forty years. He even built a laboratory there so that he could carry on working on holiday.

Aleck was always busy. In 1888, he helped his
father-in-law to set up a new society for travellers
and explorers. It was called the National Geographic
Society. He later became its president.
The society is still going strong today.

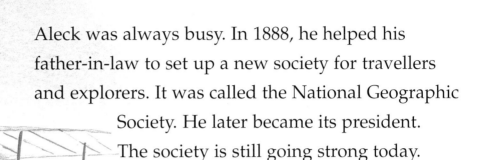

But Aleck still had one burning ambition.
He wanted to make a flying machine.
He watched the birds for hours, hoping
to learn from them. At Cape Breton,
he tested out over 30 kites and
flying machines. Even after
the first powered flight
was made by the Wright
Brothers in 1903, Aleck
did not give up. In 1908,
he and some friends
won a trophy for
building a plane
that flew further
than a kilometre.

How is Alexander Graham Bell remembered today?

On 1 August 1922, Alexander Graham Bell fell ill at his Cape Breton home. He died the next day holding Mabel's hand. He was 75 years old and had carried on working right up to the end. His funeral took place a few days later. As a sign of respect, all the telephones in the USA were silent for a minute.

By the time of Bell's death, there were millions of telephones in use in the USA, Canada and Europe. Bell's most famous invention had changed the way people communicated forever.

Today, it is possible to keep in touch with people by phone in even the most remote places, including outer space! Satellites beam phone calls all over the Earth. We use telephones to access the Internet, and mobile phones are so small that they can be tucked in a pocket. It is hard to believe that just over 125 years ago the idea of a telephone seemed too far-fetched to be true.

Bell's name will always be linked to the telephone. But he never stopped his work for the deaf. The Alexander Graham Bell Institute for the Deaf in Washington DC is still a worldwide centre for the study of hearing difficulties.

Some important dates

1847 Alexander Bell is born in Scotland.

1858 Bell briefly goes to school. He adopts the middle name Graham and becomes known as Alexander Graham Bell.

1860 Bell goes to live in London with his grandfather.

1861 Bell begins teaching in Elgin, Scotland.

1864 Bell begins helping his father demonstrate his Visible Speech system, for teaching deaf people how to speak.

1867 Bell's younger brother, Edward (Ted), dies of tuberculosis.

1869 Bell starts teaching the deaf in London.

1870 Bell's older brother, Melville (Melly), also dies of tuberculosis. The Bell family emigrate to Canada.

1871 Bell moves to Boston, USA, to teach at the School for the Deaf.

1872 Bell opens his own school for the deaf in Boston. He starts experimenting on the multiple telegraph.

1873 Bell becomes Professor of Vocal Physiology at Boston University.

1875 Thomas Watson becomes Bell's assistant. In June, they manage to transmit the sound of a plucked reed.

1876 On 7 March, Bell receives US Patent No. 174,465 for the telephone.

1876 On 10 March, the first words are heard through the telephone. In June, Bell demonstrates his telephone at the Centenary Exhibition in Philadelphia.

1877 Bell marries Mabel Hubbard. They spend their honeymoon in Britain. Bell demonstrates the telephone to Queen Victoria. In the USA, the Bell Telephone Company is formed.

1880 Bell invents the photophone. It uses light waves to send sound. France awards Bell the Volta Prize. He resigns from the Bell Telephone Company.

1881 Bell invents a metal detector and a respirator.

1888 With his father-in-law, Bell founds the National Geographic Society.

1892 Bell makes the first long-distance telephone call from New York to Chicago.

1893 Bell sets up the Association for the Promotion of Teaching Speech to the Deaf.

1897 Bell is elected president of the National Geographic Society.

1908 Bell and his friends win a prize for the first manned flight longer than a kilometre. Their plane is called the June Bug.

1915 Bell opens the first transcontinental telephone line from New York to San Francisco. He speaks to Thomas Watson.

1922 On 2 August, Bell dies. He is buried at Baddeck Bay. Every telephone in the USA falls silent for one minute.

Glossary

acid A chemical. Strong acids, such as sulphuric and nitric acids, are very dangerous because they can burn.

artificial Something that is not made or done naturally. For example, a machine is used to help people breathe artificially.

climate The general pattern and type of weather a place has over a period of time.

communicate To send information to people and places in a variety of ways, such as by voice, by letter and by telephone.

dedicated To have a very strong interest in something, such as a hobby, and to give a great deal of time and thought to it.

electric current The flow of electricity through a wire.

electromagnet A magnet made by passing electricity though a coil of wire around a bar of iron. You can switch the magnetism of an electromagnet on and off by switching the electricity on and off. Electromagnets are used in many machines including computers, telephones, and in vehicles.

elocution Being able to speak clearly and well.

hoax Something which is a fake. A hoax is a deliberate attempt to deceive, or trick, a person.

Internet The largest computer network in the world. It is made up of thousands of smaller networks, accessed by telephone line.

parchment The specially treated skin of an animal, such as a calf or sheep. Parchment used to be used for writing on instead of paper.

patent An official document that is awarded to inventors. It states that a person is the rightful inventor of an item and gives him or her the rights to their invention for a set number of years.

receiver The part of a telephone that turns your voice from an electric current back into sound. In early telephones, receivers and transmitters were separate devices. In modern telephones, the receiver and transmitter are in the handset.

remote Another word for far away or distant.

satellite An object that goes round, or orbits, the Earth. Communications satellites transmit telephone and television signals around the world.

sound waves Vibrations which travel through the air.

symbol A picture or sign which stands for something else, such as a word or sound.

transmitter The part of a telephone that sends the sound of your voice as an electric current. In early telephones, receivers and transmitters were separate devices. In modern telephones, the receiver and transmitter are in the handset.

tuberculosis A disease that affects a person's chest and lungs. It also causes fever, weakness, weight loss and severe coughing. It used to be known as consumption.

vibrate To shake or move back and forth very quickly.

vocal physiology Physiology is the scientific study of how the body works. Vocal physiology is the study of how the voice works.

Index